7+ COMPREHENSION

Practice Papers & In-Depth Guided Answers:
Volume Two

R. P. DAVIS

LAUREN BENZAKEN

Contents

Paper Eight: The Extended Concentration Paper

Note on Volume Two

Welcome to Accolade's second volume of 7+ comprehension papers.

The foreword that follows this note is largely unchanged from the foreword that appeared in the first volume, and contains all of the same "general" advice and guidance. Moreover, the way this book is structured is also much the same: eight papers, each one modelled on a different type of paper issued by the UK's top schools (as explained in more depth in the foreword). However, each of the eight papers – plus the model answers – are wholly original. And while the analyses we offer for these model answers do repeat some of the guidance that appears in Volume 1, they are of course tailored to the new answers we have provided.

Foreword

When sitting 7+ comprehension exams at top schools you will notice that, although all of their papers follow the same basic formula – an extract accompanied by a set of questions – the *types* of questions they ask can vary a good deal. The reason for this is simple enough: these schools write their papers in-house, and that means you find quirks in some papers that you don't in others. And yet, for all these quirks, there is still a *huge* degree of overlap between these various papers, because ultimately these schools are all looking for a similar set of skills.

As a result, preparing for these exams is eminently possible. We simply need to identify the various types of questions that appear (including those quirky ones!), then hone the skills required to answer them.

The intention of this guide is not simply to show you what these exams tend to look like (although, as you work through it, you will inevitably get a sense of this nonetheless!). No, the intention is to go a step further, and show you how to decode the sorts of questions these 7+ comprehension papers tend to ask, and what "perfect" answers to these questions look like. Moreover, it also seeks to explain, *in detail*, how exactly the model answers provided satisfy the examiners' criteria, making it as easy as possible for students to understand how to emulate these answers.

While we are shortly going to delve into the specific questions that appear in these papers, it is possible to itemize the skills the 7+ papers generally ask candidates to demonstrate. They almost always require students to show they can **retrieve** information from a passage, but they also, on occasion, require candidates to show they can **infer** information when it's not explicit. They often require students to show they comprehend certain **vocabulary** and pieces of **punctuation**. Not infrequently, they will want students to demonstrate their **reasoning** skills. Finally, some of these papers – though not all – want students to demonstrate their capacity for **creativity**.

Not all 7+ papers test all of these skills; but all of them will test at least some of them.

Indeed, it ought to be noted that they all base their questions on the objectives for Years 2 and 3 students set out in the English National Curriculum – these schools are ultimately looking to see how well a candidate can apply skills they've learned in class when confronted with a passage they have not encountered before.

How this book is set out.

As mentioned, 7+ papers are incredibly varied. However, if you spend enough time and energy looking through past papers, you start to figure out what makes them tick, and notice certain patterns that emerge time and again. This book contains eight papers, each written in a different "style" – and each style reflects a different type of paper one might encounter in a 7+ comprehension exam. I have labelled the eight types of papers as follows:

1. The Retrieve and Define Paper
2. The Light Inference Paper
3. The Training Wheels Paper
4. The What, Why, Where & How Paper
5. The Marks Aplenty Paper
6. The All-Rounder Paper
7. The Extended Answer Paper
8. The Extended Concentration Paper

The labels I've given each style should give you some indication of what the papers entail. It may well be the case that some of the 7+ comprehension papers you end up taking fit neatly into the one of these styles. However, it is just as possible that they wind up being a blend of two (or more) styles – after all, schools often tweak the style of paper they put out year on year. At any rate, I can assert with confidence that, if you are well versed in all eight styles, you will have your bases covered, and be prepared for most anything.

The questions for each paper appear twice. The first time they will appear is immediately after the extract, so that students can, if they wish, have a go at tackling the paper. They will then appear a second time, but this time accompanied by model answers and detailed guidance.

Each of the papers includes a "time guide" – that is, the amount of time one would expect to be given to complete the paper in an exam hall. If students wish to complete some of these papers as practice, I suspect this may prove useful.

Insofar as difficulty is concerned, these papers have been ordered from easiest to hardest, with the final few papers really seeking to stretch students' capabilities. The truth of the matter is that the difficulty of 7+ exam papers are *not* uniform: some schools set harder papers than others – and these discrepancies in difficulty exist even between top-flight schools whose papers you might expect to be pretty similar.

I feel the need at this point to clarify that my intention is *not* to intimidate by saying this. On the contrary, by exposing students to the reality of what is in store, I believe it ensures that, when it actually comes to entering the exam hall, you feel far more at ease.

There is no *correct* way to use this guide, though I would suggest it is probably sensible to have a parent at hand to act as a kind of surrogate tutor while the student works through this volume. In any case, the intention of this book is to give the reader the experience of having an experienced tutor at their beck and call.

Exam Tips

Within this book, you will find a good deal of question specific advice. However, there are a number of more general tips that it is important for any 7+ candidate to keep in mind:

- When reading the extract, don't rush. Some papers even set aside 10 minutes explicitly for reading the paper, and do not allow you to look at the questions until those 10 minutes have elapsed. This does not mean that 10 minutes is always necessary – but keep in mind that every school will expect you to read the passage very carefully.
- Read the questions carefully. It sounds obvious, I know, but you wouldn't believe how many times I have seen bright students lose marks simply because they have misread the question
- Always write in full sentences, unless you are explicitly told this is not required.
- If you are unhappy with an answer, and feel as though you must write something else, do not cross out your old answer until you have fully finished writing the new one – you may be throwing away precious marks!
- Most papers tell you how many marks a question is worth. Keep

this in mind when working out how much time to spend on any given question.

- Remember: just because a question is, for instance, worth three marks, that does not necessarily mean you need to give three separate points. Of course there *are* occasions when three marks require three points, and I shall discuss those occasions in this book – but this is not *always* the case.
- Many 7+ papers give candidates blank lines on which to compose their answers. When these appear, take them seriously: they are guidelines regarding how long the examiners would like your answer to be.

Paper One: The Retrieve and Define Paper

The questions in the Retrieve and Define Paper require candidates to flex their retrieval and definition skills. Although other skills (such as inference, reasoning, and creativity) are tested in other 7+ papers, this particular style of paper – which is probably the most basic type you will come across – revolves solely around retrieval and definitions.

The Suffragettes
THE RETRIEVE AND DEFINE PAPER; 15 MINUTES

Read the passage below and answer the questions that follow.

---

1   Until 1918, women in the UK were not allowed to vote in elections. A group of protesters, known as the suffragettes, played a key role in securing the vote for women. Perhaps the most famous suffragette was a woman called Emmeline Pankhurst. She was born in Manchester in 1858.
5   Pankhurst set up the Women's Social and Political Union (WSPU) in 1903 and was arrested many times as a result of her protests. In 1913 alone, Pankhurst was arrested thirteen times and spent 30 days in prison! Pankhurst paused her protests when World War One started in 1914 – she believed it was important to help the war effort instead. Nevertheless, the
10 government granted the vote to all women over 30 in 1918, and Pankhurst was crucial to this happening.

An extract from The Suffragettes, written by a Year 3 student.

1. Which famous protester is the passage discussing? (1)

2. Who were the suffragettes? (2)

3. The Women's Social and Political Union was set up in which year? (1)

1918	1858
1903	1914

4. How many times was Pankhurst arrested in 1913? (1)

5. Why did Pankhurst pause her protests in 1914? (2)

6. What does the word 'granted' mean? (1)

deprived	took
promised	given

Model Answers & Guidance

1. Which famous protester is the passage discussing? (1)

The passage talks about the famous protester Emmeline Pankhurst.

The paper is starting the student off gently with a simple comprehension question that tests the candidate's ability to retrieve information. Half a mark should be deducted for not using capital letters or correct punctuation, though multiple mistakes do not incur this penalty multiple times.

Students who understand the meaning of the word 'protester' will likely find this question straightforward. However, since the paragraph makes it clear that suffragettes were protesters, and that Emmeline Pankhurst was a suffragette, making the connection between the word 'protester' and Emmeline Pankhurst should be feasible for those students who are not familiar with the word, too.

Moreover, given that Emmeline Pankhurst is the only protester mentioned in the passage, students should be able to deduce the correct answer either way. *[retrieval]*

2. Who were the suffragettes? (2)

The suffragettes were a group of protesters who played a key role in getting the vote for women.

Again, the examiner is looking to see whether a student can retrieve specific information from the text to answer the question. One mark would be granted for mentioning that the suffragettes were protesters, and another for adding that they played a key part in securing the vote for women. This information can be found in lines 2-3 of the passage. *[retrieval]*

3. The Women's Social and Political Union was set up in which year? (1)

1918	1858
1903	1914

The question offers the student four different figures, and is looking to establish whether the student can link the event mentioned – the year the Women's Social and Political Union was established – to the correct set of digits. Notice that the other figures are linked to other events mentioned in the passage. It is important for students to take their time, as the examiners know that some will rush and pluck out a different (but incorrect!) date they can see in the extract. *[retrieval and multiple choice]*

4. How many times was Pankhurst arrested in 1913? (1)

Pankhurst was arrested thirteen times in 1913.

Again, this question is stretching the student's retrieval skills. On this occasion, the candidate needs to draw out the detail at line 7 – namely, that Pankhurst was arrested thirteen times in 1913.

As an aside, whenever you have a question that focuses on a particular year or date, it is often sensible to scan the text for that date, as this will often help you track down the answer.

Continue to deduct half a point if there are any punctuation or spelling mistakes. That said, if the candidate writes '13' as opposed to 'thirteen', they should *not* be penalised. *[retrieval]*

5. Why did Pankhurst pause her protests in 1914? (2)

Pankhurst paused her protests in 1914 because of the start of World War One. She believed it was more important to help with the war effort.

One mark for acknowledging that Pankhurst paused her protests in 1914 due to the outbreak of World War One, and one mark for mentioning that Pankhurst thought that helping with the war effort should be her focus instead.

This is, essentially, another retrieval question: it is a skill that has already been tested, but the examiner is making sure that the student has paid attention to the entirety of the passage. The correct answer can be found at lines 8 and 9 – and, at the risk of sounding like a broken record, deduct half a point if there are any incorrect spellings and/or punctuation errors. [*retrieval*]

6. What does the word 'granted' mean? (1)

deprived	took
promised	given

Although this is another multiple choice question, this time it is testing the student's ability to define a specific word. If the student is not familiar with the word, they should carefully re-read the sentence in which the word appears, as well as the sentences either side of it. They should then replace the word in question with each of the four options given above. This will give the student a fighting chance to make an educated guess!

At any rate, this is a good opportunity to discuss other words that mean the same as grant/give with your child. [*definitions and multiple choice*]

Paper Two: The Light Inference Paper

Inference questions tend to stretch candidates further than retrieval and definition questions. While other papers in this volume test candidates' inference skills more extensively, the gentle foray into inference we see in this paper – The Light Inference Paper – gives students a chance to acclimatise to the challenges inference-based questions present.

The Magic Nuts

THE LIGHT INFERENCE PAPER; 15 MINUTES

In this extract from the start of a novel, Leonore is riding on a train. Read the passage and answer the questions that follow.

1   Little Leonore pressed her face against the window of the railway carriage
    and tried hard to see out. But it was no use. It all looked so dark and black,
    all the darker and blacker for the glimmer of the rain-drops trickling down
    thickly outside.

5   Leonore sighed deeply with boredom. She wished with all her heart that it
    was daylight, and that she could get out of the stuffy old railway train, and
    go for a good run. They had been shut up in this train carriage for hours,
    bum-bumming along in this boring way. It even seemed to her now and
    then as if she had *always* been sitting in her corner like this, and that it had
10 *always* been night and *always* this gloomy.

    'I don't believe I'm going to be happy at all at Alten,' she said to herself.
    'I'm sure it's going to be horrid. It's always the way if people tell you

anything's going to be lovely and nice, it's sure to be dull, and—just horrid.'

15   She glanced at the other end of the railway carriage where a lady, comfortably muffled up in the corner, was sleeping peacefully. It was her nanny.

'I wish I could go to sleep like Nanny,' was the next thought that came into her busy brain.

Then her eyes fell on the little cushion and the railway rug that she had
20   thrown on to the floor—should she try to settle herself again and *perhaps* manage to go to sleep? It would be so nice to wake up and find they had arrived. Nanny had said they would arrive at Alten at ten o'clock, had she not?

An extract adapted from The Magic Nuts by Mary Louisa
Stewart Molesworth

---

1. "It all looked so dark and black, all the darker and blacker for the glimmer of the rain-drops trickling down thickly outside."

What does this sentence suggest the weather is like at the start of this extract? (1)

sunny	wet	dry

2. Circle the word that shows how Leonore is feeling while riding on the train. (1)

enthusiastic	guilty
joyous	bored

2b. Explain why she feels this way. (1)

3. Using the information in the text, put a tick in the correct box to show whether the statement is true or false. (5)

	True	False
Leonore does not know the woman in the corner.		
Leonore has been in the train for less than an hour.		
The train is headed for Alten.		
Leonore is sitting under a railway rug.		
Leonore does not have a cushion.		

4. 'Staring sadly through the gathering mist, the timid girl winced.'

Pick out two adjectives from this sentence. (2)

Model Answers & Guidance

1. "It all looked so dark and black, all the darker and blacker for the glimmer of the rain-drops trickling down thickly outside."

What does this sentence suggest the weather is like at the start of this extract? (1)

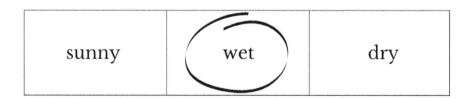

| sunny | wet | dry |

Again, as in the previous paper, we have a multiple choice question. However, this question – unlike any that appeared in the previous paper – is asking the student to make an inference.

To infer something is to "read between the lines" and deduce information that is not said explicitly. In this case, the quote mentions 'rain-drops trickling down thickly outside'. Although at no point does the passage say explicitly it is wet outside, we know that there are rain-drops on the carriage's windows, and thus we can *infer* from this that the weather is wet. [*multiple choice and inference*]

2. Circle the word that shows how Leonore is feeling while riding on the train. (1)

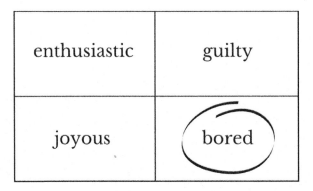

This question involves more straightforward retrieval skills. At line 5, we are told that 'Leonore sighed deeply with boredom', which makes it plain that she is feeling bored. [*multiple choice*]

2b. Explain why she feels this way. (1)

She feels bored because she has been stuck in the train for hours.

This question is slightly harder, since it requires the candidate to make a connection that is not made explicit in the passage.

As mentioned in the explanation to the previous question, we first learn that Leonore is bored at line 5. In the next sentence, we learn that she 'wished… that she could get out of the stuffy old train', which hints that her boredom stems from being stuck on the train. In the sentence after this, we learn that Leonore has been 'shut up' in the train 'for hours'. By emphasising how long Leonore has been on the train, this sentence further cements the link between her entrapment in the carriage and her boredom.

In short, to score the mark, the candidate needs to link Leonore's boredom to the fact that she has been trapped on the train *and* to the fact that she has been on the train for a sustained period of time (though the candidate does *not* necessarily need to use the word 'hours' to communicate this concept of a sustained period of time). *[retrieval and reasoning]*

3. Using the information in the text, put a tick in the correct box to show whether the statement is true or false. (5)

	True	False
Leonore does not know the woman in the corner.		✓
Leonore has been in the train for less than an hour.		✓
The train is headed for Alten.	✓	
Leonore is sitting under a railway rug.		✓
Leonore does not have a cushion.		✓

Again, the examiner is testing the candidate's retrieval skills. However, this time the student is being presented with a series of statements, and they must use their retrieval skills to establish whether the statements are correct or not.

Notice that the statements that are false will actively clash with information that can be found in the passage. For instance, we are explicitly told at lines 19-20 about Leonore's 'cushion' that is resting 'on the floor'. This makes it abundantly clear that she *does* in fact have a cushion, clashing with the fifth statement above.

4. 'Staring sadly through the gathering mist, the timid girl winced.'

Pick out two adjectives from this sentence. (2)

1. gathering

2. timid

You will sometimes get a question that is unrelated to the passage. This sort of non-passage related question, when it appears, will usually come at the end of a paper.

This question is looking to establish that the candidate understands that an adjective is a describing word. One mark for each correct adjective identified.

The word 'sadly' will likely confuse some candidates. However, 'sadly' is *not* an adjective, but an adverb. An adjective is a word that describes a noun. Yet 'sadly' here is describing the word 'staring', which is a verb. Therefore, 'sadly' is an adverb.

This is a good opportunity to talk about other words that mean the same thing as the two words above. *[vocabulary]*

Paper Three: The Training Wheels Paper

Although this paper pushes students into new territory – for instance, it gets students to start flexing their creative muscles – many of the questions have been partially written by the examiner, and simply require the candidate to fill in the blanks. Accordingly, I have dubbed this format the Training Wheels Paper.

About Bees

THE TRAINING WHEELS PAPER; 20 MINUTES

This passage offers some brief information about bees. Read the passage and answer the questions that follow.

---

1   There are three kinds of bees. The most important bee in the hive is naturally the queen. She is longer and sleeker than the others, and has a crooked sting, of which, however, she rarely makes use.

Similar in form, but smaller, are the working-bees, whose sting is straight.
5   The male bee, or drone, is thicker than the others, and stingless.

The queen is the mother-bee of the hive and lays all the eggs, and is so diligent that she usually lays twelve hundred in a day, having a separate cell for each egg. That is her only work; for she leaves the whole care of her children to the industrious working-bees, who have various labours to
10   perform. Some of them build cells of wax; others bring in honey on the dust of flowers, called pollen; yet others feed and take care of the young; and a small number act as body-guard to the queen.

Different types of bees take different amounts of time to mature from an egg. The queen requires but sixteen days in which to come to maturity;
15 while the workers require twenty, and the drones twenty-four. When several queens appear at the same time, they fight until one gains the victory.

Honey is the nectar of flowers, which bees collect with their tongues, place in their honey-bags, and deposit in cells built for the purpose, which, when
20 filled, they cover with wax.

Bees secrete wax from between the rings which form their bodies, and then work the substance with the mouth until it is fit for the construction of the comb. Bees also make a gummy substance for varnishing their cells, which they collect from the buds of trees.

Adapted from About Bees in The Nursery Vol XIII

1. Put these details in the order in which they appear in the passage. The first one has been done for you. (4)

Queen bees rarely use their sting.	
Bees make a gummy substance to use as varnish.	
Each bee egg is placed in a separate cell.	
There are three kinds of bees.	1
The male bee is thicker than the others.	

2. How many eggs do queen bees usually lay in a day? (1)

Queen bees usually lay about _____ eggs in a day.

3. Queen bees have a crooked sting. What kind of sting do working-bees have? (1)

Working bees have a _____ sting.

4. How does the male bee's sting compare to that of the queen bee and the working bee? (2)

5. Do queen bees have various labours to perform on top of laying eggs? Please answer with 'yes' or 'no'. (1)

6. Aside from bringing honey into the hive, name three other tasks that worker bees perform. (2)

Worker bees have been known to _____, _____ and _____.

7. How many days do male bees take to come to maturity? (1)

Male bees take _____ days to come to maturity.

8. Which type of bee takes sixteen days to come to maturity? (1)

9. When several queen bees appear at once, why do you think they fight each other? (2)

10. Why do you think the writer believes that the queen bees are the most important type of bee in the hive? (2)

11. With which part of their body do bees collect nectar from flowers? (1)

12. Write the name of two other types of insects you might encounter at your local park. (2)

Model Answers & Guidance

1. Put these details in the order in which they appear in the passage. The first one has been done for you. (4)

Queen bees rarely use their sting.	2
Bees make a gummy substance to use as varnish.	5
Each bee egg is placed in a separate cell.	4
There are three kinds of bees.	1
The male bee is thicker than the others.	3

This question is designed to test a candidate's alertness to the passage's structure – what order does the information appear in? Reading the passage carefully is a necessity, and the candidate will be awarded one mark for each part numbered correctly.

Encourage your child to go over their answers when they are done: candidates are most likely to make an error in this type of question when they are rushing or nervous. *[summarising]*

2. How many eggs do queen bees usually lay in a day? (1)

Queen bees usually lay about <u>twelve hundred</u> eggs in a day.

Whereas retrieval questions in previous papers have required the student to construct a full sentence by themselves, a number of questions in this paper ease the student in by writing out the sentence for the student and inviting them to fill in the blank.

Although punctuation and spelling is less likely to be an issue with the sentence partially written, do make sure that the words you add into the sentence are spelt correctly, and that any punctuation you use is correct, as if you make an error it will still cost you half a mark. That said, if a candidate here wrote "1,200" as opposed to "twelve hundred", they would still have received full marks. *[retrieval]*

3. Queen bees have a crooked sting. What kind of sting do working-bees have? (1)

Working bees have a <u>straight</u> sting.

Again we have a retrieval question with training wheels attached: the examiner has written out most of the sentence on the student's behalf. The detail the candidate is required to extract can be found at line 4. *[retrieval]*

4. How does the male bee's sting compare to that of the queen bee and the working bee? (2)

Unlike the queen bee and the working bee, the male bee is stingless.

———

We again have a question that requires the student to retrieve information; but this time the training wheels have been removed, and the student must write the entire sentence themselves.

The sentence the student produces must compare the male/drone bee to both the queen bee <u>and</u> the working bee. Remove half a mark if only one of these other two bees are mentioned. *[retrieval]*

5. Do queen bees have various labours to perform on top of laying eggs? Please answer with 'yes' or 'no'. (1)

No.

———

A straightforward retrieval question that is reminiscent of the 'True' or 'False' question in the previous paper. There is no need to write 'No, the queens do not perform various labours' as the question is explicitly asking you to answer with a single word. *[retrieval]*

6. Aside from bringing honey into the hive, name three other tasks that worker bees perform. (2)

Worker bees have been known to build cells of wax, feed and take care of the young and act as bodyguard to the queen bee.

The training wheels have returned for this question: much of the sentence has been written by the examiner.

Remove half a mark if only two tasks are mentioned, and a full mark if only one is mentioned. *[retrieval]*

7. How many days do male bees take to come to maturity? (1)

Male bees take twenty four days to come to maturity.

Again, the examiner has written out most of the sentence already.

If the candidate writes '24' instead, they will still be rewarded the mark. *[retrieval]*

8. Which type of bee takes sixteen days to come to maturity? (1)

The queen bee takes sixteen days to come to maturity.

This retrieval question is only worth the one mark as the candidate is only required to pluck out one particular detail; namely, that it is the queen bee that take sixteen days to come to maturity. *[retrieval]*

9. When several queen bees appear at once, why do you think they fight each other? (2)

I think they fight each other as they are competing to be the only queen bee in the hive, so they can lay all the eggs.

This question is slightly more tricky as it requires students to engage their reasoning skills, and even to deploy some creativity.

Some candidates may know independently that a bee hive only has one queen bee, and others may have inferred as much from the subtle hints in the passage. At any rate, candidates that coherently argue that the queens fight to be the one and only queen bee will be awarded both marks.

However, if a candidate does not demonstrate knowledge that there can only be one queen bee per hive, but still correctly argues that the queens are fighting for the right to lay the eggs, they are still entitled to both marks. *[creativity and reasoning]*

10. Why do you think the writer believes that the queen bees are the most important type of bee in the hive? (2)

The writer believes the queen bee is the most important type of bee because she is the mother bee of the hive and lays all the eggs. Without the queen, the bees would not be able to survive into the future.

The candidate will be awarded one mark for demonstrating an understanding that the queens are significant as the mother bee. Another mark will be awarded for acknowledging that, because she lays all of the eggs, she is crucial to the future survival of the hive.

This question goes beyond mere retrieval, and also requires the student to demonstrate their reasoning skills. Can they articulate *why* the queen is so important? *[retrieval and reasoning]*

11. With which part of their body do bees collect nectar from flowers? (1)

Bees collect nectar from flowers using their tongues.

This question is very similar to previous retrieval-focused questions in this paper, though this time we are being asked about the specific body part bees use to collect nectar.

The candidate must be able to identify the fact that bees use their tongues to collect nectar: a detail that can be found at line 18. *[retrieval]*

12. Write the name of two other types of insects you might encounter at your local park. (2)

At my local park I might come across ants and beetles.

Here the examiner is looking at a child's general knowledge.

Award one mark for each type of insect given, and be sure to credit any sensible answer. *[creativity]*

Paper Four: The What, Why, Where & How Paper

While this paper does contain the occasional inference and reasoning based question, it is largely a retrieval orientated paper. However, the passage is starkly more tricky than the ones we have previously encountered, and thus the retrieval tasks – which require candidates to probe into not just what happens in the narrative, but why, where and how (hence the paper's name!) – are in turn more challenging.

The Wizard of Oz

THE WHAT, WHY, WHERE & HOW PAPER; 25 MINUTES

In this extract, Dorothy wakes up in the company of her companion, Scarecrow, and her pet, Toto. Read the passage and answer the questions that follow.

----

1   When Dorothy awoke the sun was shining through the trees and Toto had long been out chasing birds around him and squirrels. She sat up and looked around her. Scarecrow, still standing patiently in his corner, waiting for her.

5   "We must go and search for water," she said to him.

"Why do you want water?" he asked.

"To wash my face, clean after the dust of the road, and to drink, so the dry bread will not stick in my throat."

"It must be inconvenient to be made of flesh," said the Scarecrow thought-
10   fully, "for you must sleep, and eat and drink. However, you have brains, and it is worth a lot of bother to be able to think properly."

They left the cottage and walked through the trees until they found a little spring of clear water, where Dorothy drank and bathed and ate her breakfast. She saw there was not much bread left in the basket, and the girl was
15 thankful the Scarecrow did not have to eat anything, for there was scarcely enough for herself and Toto for the day.

When she had finished her meal, and was about to go back to the road of yellow brick, she was startled to hear a deep groan near by.

"What was that?" she asked timidly.

20 "I cannot imagine," replied the Scarecrow; "but we can go and see."

Just then another groan reached their ears, and the sound seemed to come from behind them. They turned and walked through the forest a few steps, when Dorothy discovered something shining in a ray of sunshine that fell between the trees. She ran to the place and then stopped short, with a little
25 cry of surprise.

One of the big trees had been partly chopped through, and standing beside it, with an uplifted axe in his hands, was a man made entirely of tin. His head and arms and legs were jointed upon his body, but he stood perfectly motionless, as if he could not stir at all.

30 Dorothy looked at him in amazement, and so did the Scarecrow, while Toto barked sharply and made a snap at the tin legs, which hurt his teeth.

"Did you groan?" asked Dorothy.

"Yes," answered the tin man, "I did."

An extract from The Wizard of Oz by L. Frank Baum

1. What *two* types of animals had Toto been chasing before Dorothy woke up? (2)

2. Where is the Scarecrow standing when Dorothy wakes up? (1)

3. Why does Dorothy want to find some water? (2)

4. Where does Dorothy eat her breakfast? (1)

5. Why is Dorothy thankful that the Scarecrow does not eat food? (2)

6. Why does Dorothy not head back to the road of yellow bricks after finishing her breakfast? (2)

7. What sort of animal do you think Toto is and why do you think this? (2)

8. How does Toto hurt his teeth? (1)

9. What is the tin-man holding when Dorothy finds him, and what do you think he had been doing with this item? (2)

Model Answers & Guidance

1. What *two* types of animals had Toto been chasing before Dorothy woke up? (2)

Toto was chasing birds and squirrels before Dorothy woke up.

———

Make sure to include the <u>two</u> animals Toto had been chasing to score both marks. *[retrieval]*

2. Where is the Scarecrow standing when Dorothy wakes up? (1)

The Scarecrow is standing in the corner when Dorothy wakes up.

———

A single mark will be awarded for correctly identifying that the Scarecrow was in the corner when Dorothy woke up. Remember to scan the text for key words – such as 'awoke' or 'standing' – to help you find the answer. As ever, be sure to write in complete sentences. *[retrieval]*

3. Why does Dorothy want to find some water? (2)

Dorothy wants to find water to clean her face of dust from the road. Dorothy also wants to find water to drink along with her dry bread, which she fears will get stuck in her throat.

This is a two mark question so it requires a longer answer. The marks are for detailing the two different reasons Dorothy wishes to track down water, which are: a) that she wants to use it to wash her face of dust; and b) that she wants to have some to drink with her dry bread.

Since the passage does offer a bit of detail, candidates will be penalised if they are too brief. For instance, if when identifying the first reason Dorothy wishes to find water, a candidate merely says Dorothy "wants to wash", they will be docked half a mark. Similarly, if they say simply that Dorothy "wants water to drink" for the second reason, without giving any more detail, they will again be docked half a mark. *[retrieval]*

4. Where does Dorothy eat her breakfast? (1)

Dorothy eats her breakfast by the little spring of clear water.

It is important here that candidates identify the spring of water as the correct answer: if they simply say 'among the trees' or 'in the forest', they will not score the mark.

Encourage your child to think about where in the text they may find the answer to this question (beginning, middle or end) and then try and scan the text for key words related to the question – eating/breakfast/location – in order to find the answer. *[retrieval]*

5. Why is Dorothy thankful that the Scarecrow does not eat food? (2)

Dorothy is thankful that the Scarecrow does not eat food because she only had a small amount of bread in her basket and it was all she had to feed not only herself, but also Toto.

This is a two mark question: one mark is for identifying that Dorothy only has a small amount of bread; another is for acknowledging that she also has an obligation to give Toto some of this bread. As ever, deduct half a mark if there are spelling mistakes or punctuation errors. *[retrieval]*

6. Why does Dorothy not head back to the road of yellow brick after finishing her breakfast? (2)

Dorothy does not head back to the road of yellow brick after breakfast because she hears a groan, and the Scarecrow encourages her to go and see where it came from.

Two marks: one for acknowledging that Dorothy heard a groan that distracted her, and another mark for acknowledging the Scarecrow's role in encouraging Dorothy to investigate the noise. Had your child simply written 'Because she heard a groan', they would likely score a single mark. *[retrieval]*

7. What sort of animal do you think Toto is and why do you think this? (2)

I believe that Toto is a dog because he chases squirrels and birds, which is something dogs do. Also, he barked at the tin-man, and dogs are known to bark.

This question is slightly more tricky than others, because we are never told explicitly that Toto is a dog; rather, this is something that must be inferred from the passage.

Candidates need to offer a reasonable explanation for why they believe Toto to be a dog. The safest way to score both marks is to mention the fact that Toto is said to have barked, which is behaviour commonly associated with dogs. However if a candidate convincingly argues that Toto is a dog by mentioning only the fact that Toto chases squirrels and birds and bites the tin-man, they can still score both marks.

As an aside, in L Frank Baum's novel, Toto is indeed a dog. However, if a candidate mentions the fact that Toto barks then suggests that he is perhaps a wolf or a fox – both animals that also bark – they would still be awarded the two marks. *[retrieval and inference]*

8. How does Toto hurt his teeth? (1)

Toto hurts his teeth by biting the tin man's leg.

The answer to this is lurking in line 31, where we learn that Toto 'made a snap at the tin legs, which hurt his teeth'.

The examiner wants to see that the candidate understands what the phrase 'made a snap at the tin legs' means - namely, that is suggesting not only that Toto bit into tin, but also that the tin was the tin-man's legs. As a result, candidates who simply replicate the wording used in the passage –

that is, something like 'Toto hurt his teeth by making a snap at the tin legs' – will *not* score the mark. *[retrieval and inference]*

9. What is the tin-man holding when Dorothy finds him, and what do you think he had been doing with this item? (2)

When Dorothy finds the tin-man, he is holding an axe. I think he was using the axe to cut the tree that Dorothy sees had been partly chopped through.

This final question exercises both retrieval and reasoning skills.

The first mark is for correctly identifying that the tin man is holding an axe when Dorothy finds him. The second mark is for correctly connecting this axe to the 'partly chopped through' tree mentioned at line 26. Candidates are expected to link the fact it has been partly chopped to the fact the tin-man is holding an axe. *[retrieval and reasoning]*

Paper Five: The Marks Aplenty Paper

The Marks Aplenty Paper tests skills we have utilised in other papers – namely, retrieval, reasoning, inference, and creativity – but the paper is unique in that questions appear to be worth more marks than we might expect. We shall of course discuss what to make of this quirk as we work through the paper.

Once on a Time
THE MARKS APLENTY PAPER; 25 MINUTES

In this extract, King Merriwig of Euralia has breakfast with his daughter, Hyacinth. Read the passage and answer the questions that follow.

———————

1   King Merriwig of Euralia sat at breakfast on his castle walls. He lifted the gold cover from the gold dish in front of him, selected a trout and conveyed it carefully to his gold plate. He was a man of simple tastes, but when you have an aunt with the newly acquired gift of turning anything

5   she touches to gold, you must let her practise sometimes.

  "Ah," said the King, "here you are, my dear." He searched for his napkin, but the Princess had already kissed him lightly on the top of the head, and was sitting in her place opposite to him.

  "Good morning, Father," she said; "I'm a little late, aren't I? I've been

10   riding in the forest."

  "Any adventures?" asked the King casually.

  "Nothing, except it's a beautiful morning."

"Ah, well, perhaps the country isn't what it was. Now when I was a young man, you simply couldn't go into the forest without an adventure of some

15 sort. The extraordinary things one encountered! Witches, giants, dwarfs ——. It was there that I first met your mother," he added thoughtfully.

"I wish I remembered my mother," said Hyacinth.

The King coughed and looked at her a little nervously.

"Seventeen years ago she died, Hyacinth, when you were only six months

20 old. I have been wondering lately whether I haven't been a little selfish in leaving you motherless so long."

The Princess looked puzzled. "But it wasn't your fault, dear, that mother died."

"Oh, no, no, I'm not saying that. As you know, a dragon carried her off

25 and—well, there it was. But supposing"—he looked at her shyly—"I had married again."

The Princess was startled.

"Who?" she asked.

The King peered into his goblet. "Well," he said, "there *are* people."

An extract adapted from *Once on a Time* by A. A. Milne

---

1. Explain what the word 'selected' means. (2)

2. Name the *two* ways in which Hyacinth greets her father. (4)

3. What had Hyacinth been doing before breakfast? Please write in a full sentence. (4)

4. Name *two* things we know about Hyacinth's mother. (4)

a)

b)

5. How do we know that Hyacinth is surprised by the idea of her father getting married a second time? (4)

6. If you had to choose to be a giant, dwarf or witch, which would you choose and why? (3)

Model Answers & Guidance

1. <u>Explain what the word 'selected' means. (2)</u>

The word 'selected' means to choose or to pick. Of the food in front of him, the king has selected the trout.

You would most likely be awarded the two points for just explaining the meaning of the word. However, you can also use the text to explain a definition, as I have done above, to ensure that the examiner has no excuse to dock a mark! *[vocabulary and definitions]*

2. <u>Name the *two* ways in which Hyacinth greets her father. (4)</u>

Hyacinth greets her father by kissing him on the top of his head and also by saying good morning to him after sitting down.

You may notice that, while retrieval questions of this kind in other papers are worth two marks, on this occasion it is worth four marks. Keep in mind that 7+ exam papers are written in-house by schools, and thus the number of marks up for grabs for a similar task can differ from school to school.

The two details the examiner wants you to pick out – namely, that Hyacinth a) kisses her father on his head, and b) verbally bids him good morning – are worth one mark apiece. Two further marks are for spelling, punctuation and coherency.

Note also that by linking the two details with connectives such as 'and' and 'also' – as I have done in the exemplar answer – you show the examiner your ability to stretch sentences. *[retrieval]*

3. What had Hyacinth been doing before breakfast? Please write in a full sentence. (4)

Before breakfast, Hyacinth had been out riding her horse in the forest.

Again we have a retrieval question. And again, the question seems to be worth more marks than we might expect.

In this instance, two marks are available for correctly acknowledging that Hyacinth, prior to breakfast, had been out riding her horse in the forest. A further two marks will be awarded for correct use of spellings, punctuation and capital letters. *[retrieval]*

4. Name *two* things we know about Hyacinth's mother. (4)

a) We know that Hyacinth's mother first met Hyacinth's father in the forest.

b) We know that Hyacinth's mother was carried away by a dragon.

Two marks are at stake for each reason. The first is for correctly identifying the reason, and the second is for using correct spellings and punctuation.

Beyond the exemplar answers given above, candidates could have mentioned instead that Hyacinth's mother had passed away, or that Hyacinth's mother was married to her father. *[retrieval]*

5. How do we know that Hyacinth is surprised by the idea of her father getting married a second time? (4)

I can tell that Hyacinth is surprised by the idea of her father getting married again because she is 'startled' when her father mentions the idea and then she asks 'who?' straight after.

Two marks are for retrieving the correct evidence to demonstrate that Hyacinth is surprised by the idea of her father getting remarried – namely, that she is described as being startled, and, immediately after, she quizzes her father regarding the person he wishes to marry. Two further marks are for spelling, punctuation and coherency. Remove half a mark if there are any spelling mistakes and/or punctuation errors. *[retrieval and reasoning]*

6. If you had to choose to be a giant, dwarf or witch, which would you choose and why? (3)

I would choose to be a giant so that I could see the world from above and for everything to be smaller than me. If I was a

giant I could get around much faster and could travel to other countries without having to fly on a plane or go on a train to get there. I also think that if I was a giant I would be extremely strong and would be able to pick up houses and trees without much effort.

Here the examiner is looking to see whether the candidate can come up with something creative and can back it up with an explanation. The examiner will reward one mark for offering a plausible justification for any one of the three options, and another for arguing it convincingly. A third mark will be awarded for the overall strength and creativity of the answer.

The exemplar above likely goes above and beyond by giving *multiple* explanations, though sometimes it can be sensible to extend the answer to cover all bases.

A great activity you could do with your child is to focus on the other two options - the ones they did *not* pick - and discuss possible justifications they might have provided had they picked those options instead *[creativity and reasoning]*

Paper Six: The All-Rounder Paper

This paper requires the student to demonstrate *all* the skills we have explored thus far. Since we are being put through all of our paces, this paper has been dubbed The All-Rounder Paper.

The Book of Dragons
THE ALL-ROUNDER PAPER; 30 MINUTES

In this extract, a young girl called Effie has a mysterious creature fly into her eye. Read the passage and answer the questions that follow.

---

1   It all began with Effie's getting something in her eye. It felt something like a red-hot spark—only it seemed to have legs as well, and wings like a fly. Effie rubbed and cried—not real crying, but the kind your eye does all by itself without your being miserable inside your mind—and then she went
5   to her father to have the thing in her eye taken out. Effie's father was a doctor, so of course he knew how to take things out of eyes—he did it very cleverly with a soft paintbrush dipped in castor oil.

When he had gotten the thing out, he said: "This is *very curious*."

Effie stood holding her handkerchief to her eye, and said: "I don't believe
10   it's out." People always say this when they have had something in their eyes.

"Oh, yes—it's out," said the doctor. "Here it is, on the brush. This is very interesting."

Effie had never heard her father say that about anything that she had any
15 share in. She said: "What?"

The doctor carried the brush very carefully across the room, and held the point of it under his microscope—then he twisted the brass screws of the microscope, and looked through the top with one eye.

"Dear me," he said. "Dear, dear me! Four well-developed limbs; five toes,
20 unequal in lengths; and there are traces of wings." The creature under his eye wriggled a little in the castor oil, and he went on: "Yes; a batlike wing. A new specimen, undoubtedly. Effie, run round to the professor and ask him to be kind enough to visit for a few minutes."

"You might give me a pound, Daddy," said Effie, "because I did bring you
25 the new specimen. I took great care of it inside my eye, and my eye *does* hurt."

The doctor was so pleased with the new specimen that he gave Effie a pound, and presently the professor stepped round. He stayed for lunch, and he and the doctor quarrelled very happily all the afternoon about the
30 name and the family of the thing that had come out of Effie's eye.

An extract adapted from Edith Nesbit's The Book of Dragons

1. What does the doctor use to remove the creature from Effie's eye? (1)

2. How can you tell the creature caused Effie pain? (2)

3. Why is the phrase '*very curious*' in italics? (Line 8) (2)

4. Why does the author use an exclamation mark ("!") during the doctor's comments after the doctor first inspects the creature? ('Dear, dear me!')? (2)

5. Name three things the doctor observes about the creature he plucks from Effie's eye. (2)

6. Whom does the doctor ask Effie to fetch? (1)

7. Why does the doctor want to show other people the creature he has retrieved from Effie's eye? (1)

8. What does the word 'undoubtedly' (line 22) mean? (1)

9. Why does Effie believe she deserves a pound? (2)

10. How would you feel if a tiny dragon flew into your eye? Try and answer in as much detail as you can. (5)

11. Why do you think the doctor uses a microscope to view the creature that has flown into Effie's eye? (1)

12. Find one word from the story that means the same, or nearly the same, as the words below. (4)

- **unhappy**
- **smartly**
- **ache**
- **argued**

13. Put these words in order to make a sentence. Remember to add the capital letters and full stops.

- **the loudly girl out cried incredibly (2)**
- **felt for his he sympathy daughter (2)**
- **professor the in gasped awe (2)**

Model Answers & Guidance

1. What does the doctor use to remove the creature from Effie's eye? (1)

The doctor uses a soft paintbrush dipped in castor oil to remove the creature from Effie's eye.

Encourage your child to scan the text looking for a key word from the question – in this case 'eye' – to help them locate the answer. The mark will be gained for correctly identifying that the doctor uses a soft paintbrush dipped in castor oil. Dock half a mark if the candidate does not mention the castor oil. *[retrieval]*

2. How can you tell the creature caused Effie pain? (2)

I can tell the creature caused Effie pain because it is described as a red-hot spark that caused her to cry, and because she later tells her father that it hurt.

There are two details that tell us that the creature caused Effie pain: the fact the creature is described as a red-hot spark that caused Effie to cry (one mark) and that she later tells her father explicitly that it 'hurt' (one mark).

While this question tests retrieval skills, there is also a degree of inference at play.

Although the reader in the opening paragraph is told that the creature felt like a 'red-hot spark' and that it caused Effie to cry, we are not told explicitly that it caused her pain. Rather, this is something that needs to be *inferred* from the fact that something excessively hot would likely induce pain and from the fact that crying is often a result of pain.

The second way we can tell it caused Effie pain, however, involves more straightforward retrieval. At lines 25-26 Effie explicitly tells her father that her 'eye *does* hurt'. *[retrieval and inference]*

3. Why is the phrase *'very curious'* in italics? (Line 8) (2)

This phrase is written in italics because these are used to add emphasis and the writer wants us to understand just how interesting the doctor finds the creature.

One mark is for offering an answer that acknowledges the way the italics add emphasis. For instance, the candidate may say it communicates how interesting the doctor finds the creature (as I have above). Alternatively, they may say that it shows that the doctor had wanted to emphasise what he was saying to Effie, so that she would pay attention to the creature, too.

The second mark is for writing the answer coherently and in a complete sentence.

In any case, take this as an opportunity to talk to your child about other reasons why a writer might use italics: for example, to represent a character's internal thoughts, or when voices in a story emanate from an external source - such as a radio or television.

4. Why does the author use an exclamation mark ("!") during the doctor's comments after the doctor first inspects the creature? ('Dear, dear me!')? (2)

The author uses an exclamation mark in order to communicate the doctor's shock. He is surprised and taken aback by what he can see through the microscope.

Here the examiner is looking to see whether the candidate understands how different punctuation is used and its purpose. Award one mark for a simple answer – e.g. 'The exclamation indicates the doctor's shock' – and two for writing it in a complete sentence (as shown above). *[punctuation]*

5. Name three things the doctor observes about the creature he plucks from Effie's eye. (2)

The doctor observes that the creature has four well-developed limbs, five unequal length toes, and the outline of wings.

Children can lose valuable marks by misreading questions and not double checking their answers. Encourage your child to underline how many things a question is asking for, and then check that they have met this request.

To score both marks, all three things included in my exemplar answer must feature in the candidate's answer. Two correct items will gain the candidate one and a half marks. One correct item in isolation is worth just half a mark. *[retrieval]*

6. <u>Whom does the doctor ask Effie to fetch? (1)</u>

The doctor asks Effie to fetch the professor.

This question requires simple retrieval, and the answer can be found at lines 22-23.

Remember that examiners will be looking at spelling, punctuation and grammar throughout, so make sure to use capital letters in the right places. Notice how I capitalise Effie's name, because it is a proper noun. *[retrieval]*

7. <u>Why does the doctor want to show other people the creature he has retrieved from Effie's eye? (1)</u>

The doctor wants to show other people the creature because he believes it is a previously undiscovered creature. I know this because the doctor calls it a new specimen.

This question requires very light inference, for the passage does not explicitly say that the doctor wants Effie to fetch the professor because he believes he has discovered a new creature. Instead, the passage hints that this is the reason by having the doctor tell Effie to get the professor in the sentence immediately after calling the creature 'a new specimen'.

The candidate can use the same wording as appears in the passage, and say the doctor believes he has found 'a new specimen', or they can put the answer in their own words. In my example answer, I have in fact done both, just so that the examiner has no excuse to dock a mark! *[retrieval and inference]*

8. What does the word 'undoubtedly' (line 22) mean? (1)

The word undoubtedly means without a doubt or with complete certainty.

Break down the word 'undoubtedly' with your child. The word doubt is contained within it, and your child likely knows what it means. Indicate how the "un" prefix reverses the meaning, so that the word refers to a *lack* or *absence* of doubt. Often this granular approach of breaking down longer words can help candidates make educated guesses with regards to definitions. *[vocabulary and definitions]*

9. Why does Effie believe she deserves a pound? (2)

Effie believes she deserves a pound because, if it was not for her getting the creature caught in her eye, her father would not have found the new creature. Also, she believes that the pain she went through also means she deserves a pound.

This is a two mark question, so it requires a slightly longer answer.

The first mark is for acknowledging that the central reason Effie believes she deserves a pound is because she was instrumental in her father's discovery of a new creature. The second mark is for acknowledging that she also believed that the pain she endured meant she deserves the pound. *[retrieval and reasoning]*

10. How would you feel if a tiny dragon flew into your eye? Try and answer in as much detail as you can. (5)

If a dragon flew into my eye I would feel quite scared to begin with but then I think I would find it exciting. It would be fun to have a pet dragon and interesting to see it grow over time from a tiny dragon to a big one. In addition, I would be able to take it for a walk around the park and show it to all of my friends who would be really impressed. Once my dragon grew larger, I could ride on it and we could explore the world and go on adventures.

Marks are awarded for use of correct punctuation and spelling as well as the use of interesting vocabulary and descriptive language. Using the phrase 'in addition' shows the examiner you can accretively add ideas (other useful words that achieve this include 'moreover' and 'furthermore'. A good tactic with a question like this is to first make a statement, and then to explain your answer. *[reasoning and creativity]*

11. Why do you think the doctor uses a microscope to view the creature that has flown into Effie's eye? (1)

I think the doctor used a microscope to view the creature that flew into Effie's eye because it was very small and the microscope allowed him to see it more clearly.

This question requires students to engage their reasoning and inference muscles, as the answer is not explicitly stated in the passage. Rather, students need to demonstrate that they understand that microscopes are used to view things that are too small to be seen clearly - and to infer, therefore, that the doctor used the microscope because the creature was too small to be seen clearly otherwise.

To score the mark, the candidate must cover all of these ideas in a clear and coherent fashion *[reasoning and inference]*

12. Find one word from the story that means the same, or nearly the same, as the words below. (4)

a) unhappy

miserable

b) smartly

cleverly

c) ache

hurt

d) argued

quarrelled

One mark for each correct answer.

A good way to save time flicking back and forth between a question like this and the passage itself is to make a note of the words you are being asked to find synonyms for on the page the passage is printed on. *[vocabulary and definitions]*

13. Put these words in order to make a sentence. Remember to add the capital letters and full stops.

a) the loudly girl out cried incredibly (2)

The girl cried out incredibly loudly.

b) felt for his he sympathy daughter (2)

He felt sympathy for his daughter.

c) professor the in gasped awe (2)

The professor gasped in awe.

One mark would be awarded for use of capital letters and full stops, and one for the words being placed in the correct order. *[punctuation]*

Paper Seven: The Extended Answer Paper

This paper has been labelled The Extended Answer Paper because, while many of the questions are reminiscent of questions we have encountered already, the very final question is worth 15 marks, and requires something akin to a miniature essay. While such questions are rare in 7+ papers, they do occasionally arise, and present their own unique challenges.

An Unexpected Visit

THE EXTENDED ANSWER QUESTION; 40 MINUTES

In this extract, Samir and his sister receive a visit from a neighbour. Read the passage and answer the questions that follow.

---

1   There was a sharp knock on the door. Then another.

Samir locked eyes with his younger sister.

'It's the woman from upstairs,' Hemini hissed.

Just as Samir gave a solemn nod, the knocking came yet again – this time
5   accompanied by a shrill, angry voice: 'I know you kids are in there. Open
up *this instant.*'

'Don't go,' Hemini rasped, her brown eyes bulging. 'She's a *witch*: she looks
like the one from that Youtube video. She's –'

But like a soldier accepting his fate, Samir simply marched over to the
10   door and gingerly pulled it open.

Under a wild nest of hair was the beetroot-red face of Old Woman Maloney. A bright blue vein throbbed above her glasses. 'The pair of you – I can't believe the *racket* you've been making! Your parents told me you'd be quiet as mice, but *crash, crash, crash*.'

15   Samir gulped, then glanced over his shoulder. Hemini was peeking out from behind the coat-stand.

Playing cricket inside had seemed like a good idea. But now, not only was his mother's vase broken, but Old Woman Maloney was steaming mad.

'It's not just loud, it's *selfish*. How can anyone expect to get any rest? It's a
20   Sunday, don't you know. And yes' – the woman extended a trembling index finger at Hemini, her black dressing gown looking like the Grim Reaper's robe – 'I'm talking to you, too, young lady.'

Samir knew witches didn't exist, but Mrs Maloney was *still* terrifying.

And besides, *she* was the selfish one. It was raining outside. Shouldn't kids
25   be allowed to enjoy the weekend, too?

'I'm – I'm sorry,' Samir stuttered, hoping he might appease his unwanted guest.

'Sorry!' Maloney interjected. 'When your parents hear about this, *then* you'll be sorry'

30   Samir hung his head. All he could think about was what his parents would say. After all, they *had* told them to be on their best behaviour.

'You know, it's not so easy, it's really not…'

Samir looked up. There was something suddenly different about Maloney's tone. She no longer sounded angry. She sounded sad,
35   exhausted.

'My husband… he's so sick. I don't *want* to be here shouting.' She shook her head. There were now tears swelling in her eyes, and she no longer seemed to be talking to the children. 'He just needs his rest. He's so weak.' She rested a hand against the doorframe, as if suddenly needing to prop herself up.

40

Samir opened his mouth then closed it again. They'd lived in the apartment below Old Woman Maloney for nearly six months. He had no idea she had a husband.

An extract from An Unexpected Visit by Raphael Eliyahu

---

1. What is the name of Samir's sister, and what colour eyes does she have? (2)

2. Where did Samir's sister see a witch that looked like Mrs Maloney? (1)

3. What do you think was responsible for the '*crash, crash, crash*' Maloney said she could hear? (2)

4. How do Samir and his sister behave differently to one another during this encounter with Maloney? (4)

5. At line 19, Maloney describes Samir and his sister as 'selfish'. Do you think this is true? (3)

6. Which finger does Maloney point at Samir's sister? (1)

7. Where is Samir's family's apartment located in relation to Maloney's? (1)

8. What two things do we know Maloney is wearing? (2)

9. What do you think the phrase 'hoping he might appease his unwanted guest' means? (2)

10. Read the whole passage again.

What does it tell you about the sort of person Maloney is? (Choose words from the passage to explain your views.)

You might consider her body-language, words, behaviour, and how others respond to her. (15)

Model Answers & Guidance

1. What is the name of Samir's sister, and what colour eyes does she have? (2)

Samir's sister's name is Hemini and she has brown eyes.

One mark is for identifying that Samir's sister is called Hemini, and another is for identifying that her eyes are brown.

Take off half a mark for spelling mistakes and missing punctuation. *[retrieval]*

2. Where did Samir's sister see a witch that looked like Mrs Maloney? (1)

Hemini saw a witch that looked like Mrs Maloney on a YouTube video.

To get the mark, the candidate must correctly state that a Youtube video had been the place where Hemini had seen a witch that looked like Mrs Maloney. Take off half a mark for spelling mistakes and punctuation errors. *[retrieval]*

3. What do you think was responsible for the '*crash, crash, crash*' Maloney said she could hear? (2)

I think the game of cricket that Samir and Hemini were playing and the moment the vase was broken could have been what was responsible for the crashing noise.

The first mark is for inferring that the cricket the children were playing was a likely cause of the noise Maloney could hear. The second is for mentioning the fact the children broke their mother's vase, and that this very likely also contributed to the crashing noise Mrs Maloney heard. As ever, answer the question with a full sentence explaining your answer fully. *[inference]*

4. How do Samir and his sister behave differently to one another during this encounter with Maloney? (4)

Samir is more brave during the encounter, as he is the one that opens the door, and actually talks with his angry neighbour. Hemini, on the other hand, behaves in a more fearful way. First, she tells Samir not to open the door. Later, she hides behind the coat-stand.

Award two marks for saying that Samir and Hemini differ in the degree of courage and fear they display during the encounter. Another two marks can be earned for explaining your answer – the candidate should offer at least one example that illustrates Samir's bravery (one mark), and at least one that illustrates Hemini's fear (one mark). Note that although in the example answer above I have given *two* examples for each child, this is likely more than would have been required to secure the two marks. *[retrieval and inference]*

5. At line 19, Maloney describes Samir and his sister as 'selfish'. Do you think this is true? (3)

I do not think they are selfish. Samir and his sister just wanted to be able to play cricket and they could not do so outside because it was raining.

OR

I think that Samir and his sister were selfish because they did not think about the noise they would be making when they played cricket and how it would disturb their neighbours.

This is a matter of opinion, but you will be awarded marks for explaining why you feel this statement is true or not. The candidate will score one mark for giving a verdict on the statement; another for explaining their answer in a coherent, plausible way; and another for their structure and spelling.

6. Which finger does Maloney point at Samir's sister? (1)

Maloney pointed her index finger at Samir's sister.

Yet another retrieval-based question. It is worth just one mark, and, accordingly, we only need to extract one detail – namely, that Maloney points her index finger at Hemini. *[retrieval]*

7. Where is Samir's family's apartment located in relation to Maloney's? (1)

Samir's family lived in the apartment below Maloney's.

These retrieval questions might at times seem relentless, but in essence the examiner is trying to gauge whether a candidate is paying attention to the entirety of the passage, and not just certain parts. The answer to this question, for example, is in the final sentence of the passage; so a candidate whose concentration might have tapered off towards the end of the passage might have missed it.

Remember, treat every section of the passage with the same degree of care, for questions can easily (and often do!) focus on the final sentences. *[retrieval]*

8. What two things do we know Maloney is wearing? (2)

Maloney wore glasses and a black dressing gown.

This is a slightly trickier retrieval question, as the two items of clothing the candidate is expected to extract are located in different parts of the extract. The first mark is for correctly noting that she is wearing glasses (line 12); the second is for noting that she is also wearing a black dressing gown (line 21).

As an aside, if (as part of a full sentence) a candidate had simply written 'a dressing gown' as opposed to 'a black dressing gown', they likely would have still secured that second mark. However, I would recommend adding the extra details to give the examiner no excuse to dock a half mark. *[retrieval]*

9. What do you think the phrase 'hoping he might appease his unwanted guest' means? (2)

The phrase means that Samir was hoping to please Mrs Maloney with his apology so she would leave because he did not want her to visit them.

Discuss what the word 'appease' means if your child does not already know it already. One mark for mentioning that Samir hoped his apology would satisfy Mrs Maloney; the second for mentioning that he hopes it will convince her to leave, as he had not wanted her visiting their apartment in the first place. *[vocabulary and reasoning]*

10. Read the whole passage again.

What does it tell you about the sort of person Maloney is? (Choose words from the passage to explain your views.)

You might consider her body-language, words, behaviour, and how others respond to her. (15)

We can tell that Mrs Maloney is a passionate but also short tempered woman. The intensity of her passion can be seen in the way she repeatedly knocks on the door, but also in how she tells the children to open it up. She tells them to 'Open up *this instant*', the italics showing passion. Yet her passion can also be seen as short-temperedness. When Samir says sorry, she

interrupts him and threatens him, which could be seen as overly angry.

When Samir opens the door to Mrs Maloney, the first thing he mentions is her 'wild nest of hair' and 'beetroot-red' face. This tells me that Mrs Maloney has a messy appearance, and one that is even a bit funny because it is so intense. The 'bright blue vein' that 'throbbed' adds to her funny and chaotic appearance.

Although Mrs Maloney might look funny and ridiculous, she is seen as scary by the children. We know this because early on Hemini says she looks like a 'witch', and later she is compared to the 'Grim Reaper', who represents death. Also, Samir even describes her as 'terrifying'.

Mrs Maloney does not care about the children's feelings. She does not consider the fact that it is 'raining' outside and that the children should be 'allowed to enjoy the weekend'. However, Mrs Maloney is not a selfish person because she does care about her sick husband, who 'needs his rest'.

Finally, Mrs Maloney is also quite a vulnerable person. After shouting, she is described as 'sad' and there are 'tears' in her eyes. Also, she leans on the door 'as if suddenly needing to prop herself up'. This tells me that she is vulnerable and tired because of all the effort she puts into looking after her sick husband.

Marks will be awarded based on reference to the text, explanation of your answers, use of creative vocabulary, punctuation and spelling. The examiner is looking for candidates to draw on things explicitly mentioned about

Mrs Maloney, but also on things you can *infer* from her actions and those of others around her, and to quote these in your answer.

The best way to tackle an extended answer like this is to break things down into *themes* and put together a very quick plan in advance. This may sound scary, but it is in fact a way of making our life far easier.

Before writing the answer above, I made a list of the different qualities I could see in Mrs Maloney – that is, my themes – and it looked like this:

1. Passionate / short-tempered
2. Messy / funny appearance
3. Scary to children
4. Caring towards her husband. Not caring towards the children
5. Vulnerable

Each 'theme' then became one of the paragraphs in my answer. Since I made this plan in advance, the question became far easier to write, as I knew where it was going! If each theme/paragraph scores us three marks, we are on course to pick up the fifteen marks.

It should be added that to score all fifteen marks the student *must* include quotes from the passage – after all, the question explicitly tells us to 'choose words from the passage.' Note, however, that my quotes are never more than eight words in length at the absolute longest, and most are far shorter. Notice also how they are usually integrated into a sentence. Encourage candidates to include quotes in this style as opposed to simply dropping them in as standalone sentences. *[retrieval, inference and reasoning]*

Paper Eight: The Extended Concentration Paper

The extract this paper revolves around is far longer than any other passage we have seen thus far, and the questions are far more numerous. As a result, this paper makes demands on a candidate's concentration that others do not. Accordingly, it has been labelled The Extended Concentration Paper.

The Tale of Peter Rabbit

This extract is taken from the start of a story that looks at the lives led by rabbits. Read the passage and answer the questions that follow.

1   Once upon a time there were four little Rabbits, and their names were—
Flopsy, Mopsy, Cotton-tail, and Peter. They lived with their Mother in a
sand-bank, underneath the root of a very big fir-tree.

"Now, my dears," said old Mrs. Rabbit one morning, "you may go into the
5   fields or down the lane or into the brook, but don't go into Mr. McGregor's
garden: your Father had an accident there; he was put in a pie by Mrs.
McGregor."

"Now run along, and don't get into mischief. I am going out."

Then old Mrs. Rabbit took a basket and her umbrella, and went through
10   the wood to the baker's. She bought a loaf of brown bread and five
currant buns.

Flopsy, Mopsy, and Cotton-tail, who were good little bunnies, went down the lane to gather blackberries.

But Peter, who was very naughty, ran straight away to Mr. McGregor's
15 garden, and squeezed under the gate!

First he ate some lettuces and some French beans; and then he ate some radishes.

And then, feeling rather sick, he went to look for some parsley.

But round the end of a cucumber frame, whom should he meet but Mr.
20 McGregor!

Mr. McGregor was on his hands and knees planting out young cabbages, but he jumped up and ran after Peter, waving a rake and calling out, "Stop thief."

Peter was most dreadfully frightened; he rushed all over the garden, for he
25 had forgotten the way back to the gate.

He lost one of his shoes among the cabbages, and the other shoe amongst the potatoes.

After losing them, he ran on four legs and went faster, so that I think he might have got away altogether if he had not unfortunately run into a
30 gooseberry net, and got caught by the large buttons on his jacket. It was a blue jacket with brass buttons, quite new.

Peter gave himself up for lost, and shed big tears; but his sobs were over-heard by some friendly sparrows, who flew to him in great excitement, and implored him to exert himself.

35 Mr. McGregor came up with a sieve, which he intended to pop upon the top of Peter; but Peter wriggled out just in time, leaving his jacket behind him.

And rushed into the toolshed, and jumped into a can. It would have been a beautiful thing to hide in, if it had not had so much water in it.

40 Mr. McGregor was quite sure that Peter was somewhere in the toolshed, perhaps hidden underneath a flower- pot. He began to turn them over carefully, looking under each.

Presently Peter sneezed— "Kertyschoo!" Mr. McGregor was after him in no time, and tried to put his foot upon Peter, who jumped out of a window,
45 upsetting three plants. The window was too small for Mr. McGregor, and he was tired of running after Peter. He went back to his work.

Peter sat down to rest; he was out of breath and trembling with fright, and he had not the least idea which way to go. Also he was very damp with sitting in that can.

50 After a time he began to wander about, going lippity—lippity—not very fast, and looking all around.

He found a door in a wall; but it was locked, and there was no room for a fat little rabbit to squeeze underneath.

An old mouse was running in and out over the stone doorstep, carrying
55 peas and beans to her family in the wood. Peter asked her the way to the gate, but she had such a large pea in her mouth that she could not answer. She only shook her head at him. Peter began to cry.

Then he tried to find his way straight across the garden, but he became more and more puzzled. Presently, he came to a pond where Mr.
60 McGregor filled his water-cans. A white cat was staring at some goldfish; she sat very, very still, but now and then the tip of her tail twitched as if it were alive. Peter thought it best to go away without speaking to her; he has heard about cats from his cousin, little Benjamin Bunny.

He went back towards the toolshed, but suddenly, quite close to him, he
65 heard the noise of a hoe— scr-r-ritch, scratch, scratch, scritch. Peter scut- tered underneath the bushes. But presently, as nothing happened, he came

out, and climbed upon a wheelbarrow, and peeped over. The first thing he saw was Mr. McGregor hoeing onions. His back was turned towards Peter, and beyond him was the gate!

70   Peter got down very quietly off the wheelbarrow, and started running as fast as he could go, along a straight walk behind some black-currant bushes.

Mr. McGregor caught sight of him at the corner, but Peter did not care. He slipped underneath the gate, and was safe at last in the wood outside
75   the garden.

Mr. McGregor hung up the little jacket and the shoes for a scare-crow to frighten the blackbirds.

Peter never stopped running or looked behind him till he got home to the big fir-tree.

80   He was so tired that he flopped down upon the nice soft sand on the floor of the rabbit-hole, and shut his eyes. His mother was busy cooking; she wondered what he had done with his clothes. It was the second little jacket and pair of shoes that Peter had lost in a fortnight!

An extract adapted from The Tale of Peter Rabbit by Beatrix Potter

1. Choose one answer for each question. (4)

How many rabbits in total lived together in the sand-bank?	four	five	six
What type of tree do the rabbits live under?	oak tree	fir tree	apple tree
What kind of bread does Mrs. Rabbit buy at the market?	white bread	brown bread	rye bread
What time of day does Mrs. Rabbit head to the market?	morning	afternoon	evening

2. Name three locations that Mrs. Rabbit tells the younger rabbits they are allowed to explore. (3)

3. At lines 21-22, Mr. McGregor notices Peter in his garden. What other things happened *before* this occurred? Put a circle around all the correct answers. (2)

Flopsy, Mopsy and Cotton-tail went to gather fruit
Peter ate some young cabbages
Peter ate some French beans
Peter broke a cucumber frame
Peter lost his shoes

4. How did Peter feel immediately after Mr. McGregor noticed him in the garden? Draw a circle around one correct answer. (1)

scared	excited
jealous	bored

5. Here are some things you might say about the story. Some are right, some are wrong and for some you can't tell. (4)

(TICK THE BOX THAT YOU THINK IS **CORRECT**)

	Right	Wrong	Can't tell
Peter's father was killed by Mr. McGregor			
Mrs. Rabbit does not own an umbrella.			
Peter squeezed under the gate at Mr. McGregor's garden			
Peter had never been to Mr. McGregor's garden before.			

6. Read the sentences below then number them in the correct order in which they appear in the story. Use the numbers 1, 2, 3, 4, 5, 6 and 7. The first one is done for you. (6)

Peter got caught in a gooseberry net.	
Peter encounters a cat by the pond.	
An old mouse shook her head at Peter.	
Mrs. Rabbit tells her children not to visit Mr. McGregor's garden.	1
Peter jumped into a can in the toolshed	
Mr. McGregor was hoeing onions.	
Peter went looking for parsley.	

Answer the following questions in your own words using full sentences

7. How many currant buns does Mrs. Rabbit buy at the bakery? (2)

8. In your own words, describe how Mr. McGregor reacted when he first saw Peter in his garden. (4)

9a. How did Peter feel about the cat by the pond? (1)

9b. Why did he feel like this? (2)

10. Why did Peter climb up on the wheelbarrow? (2)

11. How did Peter's feelings about Mr. McGregor's garden change from the beginning to the end of the story? (2)

11b. Why did Peter's feelings change? Explain your answer fully. (5)

Model Answers & Guidance

1. Choose one answer for each question. (4)

How many rabbits in total lived together in the sand-bank?	four	(five)	six
What type of tree do the rabbits live under?	oak tree	(fir tree)	apple tree
What kind of bread does Mrs. Rabbit buy at the market?	white bread	(brown bread)	rye bread
What time of day does Mrs. Rabbit head to the market?	(morning)	afternoon	evening

One mark for each correct answer.

This question is entirely testing the candidate's retrieval skills. So long as the candidate is prepared to read the passage carefully, and be attentive to details, they should be able to deduce all of these answers. *[retrieval and multiple choice]*

2. Name three locations that Mrs. Rabbit tells the younger rabbits they are allowed to explore. (3)

Mrs Rabbit tells the younger rabbits they are allowed to go into the fields, down the lane or into the brook.

One mark would be awarded for each correct answer - the examiner is looking for candidates to mention the fields (1 mark), down the lane (1 mark) and the brook (1 mark). Deduct half a mark for any grammatical or spelling mistakes. *[retrieval]*

3. At lines 21-22, Mr. McGregor notices Peter in his garden. What other things happened *before* this occurred? Put a circle around all the correct answers. (2)

(Flopsy, Mopsy and Cotton-tail went to gather fruit)
Peter ate some young cabbages
(Peter ate some French beans)
Peter broke a cucumber frame
Peter lost his shoes

Two marks are awarded here – one for each correct answer. It is important candidates take note that the question is asking for things that happened *before* Mr McGregor noticed Peter in his garden *[retrieval and multiple choice]*

4. How did Peter feel immediately after Mr. McGregor noticed him in the garden? Draw a circle around one correct answer. (1)

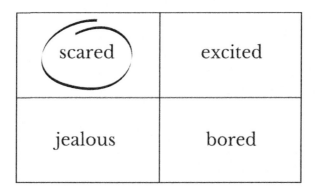

scared	excited
jealous	bored

The examiner is looking to see that the candidate can pick out a word that evokes something similar to the words used to describe Peter's feelings in the text. We are told at line 24 that 'Peter was most dreadfully frightened'. The closest word of the four we are given to describe this moment is 'scared' *[multiple choice and definitions]*

5. Here are some things you might say about the story. Some are right, some are wrong and for some you can't tell. (4)

(TICK THE BOX THAT YOU THINK IS CORRECT)

	Right	Wrong	Can't tell
Peter's father was killed by Mr. McGregor			✓ Peter's father 'had an accident' in Mr. McGregor's garden, but we don't know if McGregor killed him.
Mrs. Rabbit does not own an umbrella.		✓ We are explicitly told that 'Mrs. Rabbit took a basket and her umbrella', so she does own an umbrella.	
Peter squeezed under the gate at Mr. McGregor's garden	✓ Peter went to Mr. McGregor's garden, 'and squeezed under the gate'.		
Peter had never been to Mr. McGregor's garden before.			✓ At no point do we learn whether Peter had been to the garden before.

This style of question is very similar to a question in a previous paper that offered a set of statements and asked us whether they were true or false. Encourage your child to scan the text for key words – such as father, umbrella, gate and garden – to help them find the answers.

I have included details in my answers above regarding how I came to the answers, though a candidate would *not* need to do this to score the marks. One mark for each correct answer. *[retrieval]*

6. Read the sentences below then number them in the correct order in which they appear in the story. Use the numbers 1, 2, 3, 4, 5, 6 and 7. The first one is done for you. (6)

Peter got caught in a gooseberry net.	3
Peter encounters a cat by the pond.	6
An old mouse shook her head at Peter.	5
Mrs. Rabbit tells her children not to visit Mr. McGregor's garden.	1
Peter jumped into a can in the toolshed	4
Mr. McGregor was hoeing onions.	7
Peter went looking for parsley.	2

When your child is done numbering the sentences, encourage them to read the sentences in the order they have put them in and check that the order makes sense. *[summarising]*

Answer the following questions in your own words using full sentences

7. How many currant buns does Mrs. Rabbit buy at the bakery? (2)

Mrs Rabbit purchases five currant buns during her visit to the bakery.

One mark for the correct answer and one for correct spelling and punctuation. *[retrieval]*

8. In your own words, describe how Mr. McGregor reacted when he first saw Peter in his garden. (4)

When Mr McGregor spotted Peter in the garden for the first time, he stopped tending to his vegetables and chased after Peter with his rake, while also accusing Peter of stealing from his garden.

One mark for the correct answer; one for using original vocabulary that differs from how the author describes Mr McGregor's reaction in the passage; two marks for correct punctuation and spelling.

If the candidate simply writes the sequence identically to how it appears in the passage, they will be capped at one mark in total. *[retrieval]*

9a. How did Peter feel about the cat by the pond? (1)

Peter felt cautious towards the cat by the pond.

This is a slightly tricky question, because it requires us to read between the lines. We are told at lines 62-63 that Peter 'thought it best to go away without speaking to' the cat because he had 'heard about cats from his cousin, little Benjamin Bunny.'

Although it is not spelt out explicitly, we can infer from this that Peter, as a result of what he has heard from his cousin, feels cautious about cats, including this one. *[retrieval and inference]*.

9b. Why did he feel like this? (2)

Peter felt cautious with regards to the cat because of things he had been told about cats by his relative, Benjamin Bunny.

We in fact covered the crux of this question in the explanation to the previous one: Peter Rabbit feels cautious because of what he has been told by his cousin.

One mark is available for explaining this; and one mark is for proper sentence construction. *[retrieval and reasoning]*

10. Why did Peter climb up on the wheelbarrow? (2)

Peter clambered up the wheelbarrow in order to get a better view of the garden.

Again, this is not explicitly spelt out in the extract. Rather, we can see that Peter climbs the wheelbarrow and then is able to get a good view of Mr McGregor. From this we can infer that he climbed it in order to obtain this better view. *[retrieval and inference]*.

11. How did Peter's feelings about Mr. McGregor's garden change from the beginning to the end of the story? (2)

At the start of the story Peter was not scared at all about visiting Mr McGregor's garden and was curious about going in there. By the end of the story Peter seems like he never wants to go back to the garden ever again because he runs

away and does not look back as he is so scared of Mr McGregor.

We are not told explicitly how Peter felt at the start of the story, but we can tell he is not scared because the first thing Peter does after his mother warns him not to visit Mr McGregor's garden is go and visit it anyway. By the end of the extract, however, Peter is running away from Mr McGregor and is frantic about finding his way home. From this we can tell he is scared and is *not* looking to go back to the garden anytime soon.

One mark for talking about Peter's feelings at the start of the story and one mark for talking about his feelings at the end of the story. Dock half a mark if there are any grammatical/spelling/punctuation errors. *[retrieval and inference]*.

<u>11b. Why did Peter's feelings change? Explain your answer fully. (5)</u>

Peter's feelings changed because he did not realise at the start of the story just how frightening Mr McGregor can be and how dangerous it is to go and visit his garden. He also struggles to find his way out of the garden which causes him a lot of stress and panic. Moreover, he encounters a cat in the garden, which makes him feel even more cautious about it. At the beginning of the story Peter is not aware of all this and so he eats the vegetables in Mr McGregor's garden without a care in the world.

The examiner is looking to see whether you really understand the story and can make sense of what you have read.

Acknowledging that Peter's feelings had gone from positive to negative because of his unpleasant experience in the garden will score the candidate three marks. An extra mark can be claimed by giving specific details about what he found unpleasant in the garden - such as the fact he could not find his way out, or his encounter with the menacing cat, or Mr McGregor's angry reaction to his presence. The final mark is for the coherency of the answer as well as accurate use of connectives and punctuation. *[retrieval and reasoning]*

Printed in Great Britain
by Amazon

48394035R10064